2O__ - 2O__

Troop Leader Planner

Troop No.: _____

CONTENTS

TROOP INFORMATION
◆ LEADER _____ 1
◆ Co LEADERS AND VOLUNTEERS _____ 2
◆ TROOP ROSTER _____ 6
◆ EMAIL SHEET _____ 9
◆ HEALTH INFO _____ 11
◆ BIRTHDAY TRACKER _____ 13

CALENDARS
◆ ONE MONTH PER PAGE (JAN - AUG) _____ 15

PLANNERS & TRACKERS
◆ ATTENDANCE TRACKER _____ 35
◆ MEETING / EVENT PLANNER _____ 39
◆ BADGE AND PATCH TRACKER _____ 70
◆ FORMS AND PAPERWORK TRACKER _____ 72

FINANCES
◆ TROOP DUES AND FEES TRACKER _____ 74
◆ FINANCIAL LEDGER _____ 78
◆ CHECKING ACCOUNT TRACKER _____ 82

PRODUCT SALES
◆ INDIVIDUAL GIRLS' PRODUCT SALES TRACKER ____ 86
◆ BOOTH SALES TRACKER _____ 92

EXTRA
◆ SNACK SIGNUP SHEET _____ 104
◆ VOLUNTEER SIGNUP SHEET _____ 106
◆ NOTES AND TO-DO LIST _____ 110

LEADER

NAME:

PHONE No.:   BACKGROUND CHECKED: Yes / No

D.O.B. (date of birth)

ADDRESS:

EMAIL ADDRESS:

NOTES:

Co LEADERS AND VOLUNTEERS

NAME:

PHONE No.:   BACKGROUND CHECKED: Yes / No

D.O.B. (date of birth):

ADDRESS:

EMAIL ADDRESS:

NOTES:

◆

NAME:

PHONE No.:   BACKGROUND CHECKED: Yes / No

D.O.B. (date of birth):

ADDRESS:

EMAIL ADDRESS:

NOTES:

◆

NAME:

PHONE No.:   BACKGROUND CHECKED: Yes / No

D.O.B. (date of birth):

ADDRESS:

EMAIL ADDRESS:

NOTES:

◆

NAME:

PHONE No.:   BACKGROUND CHECKED: Yes / No

D.O.B. (date of birth):

ADDRESS:

EMAIL ADDRESS:

NOTES:

Co LEADERS AND VOLUNTEERS

NAME:

PHONE No.:   BACKGROUND CHECKED: Yes / No

D.O.B. (date of birth):

ADDRESS:

EMAIL ADDRESS:

NOTES:

NAME:

PHONE No.:   BACKGROUND CHECKED: Yes / No

D.O.B. (date of birth):

ADDRESS:

EMAIL ADDRESS:

NOTES:

NAME:

PHONE No.:   BACKGROUND CHECKED: Yes / No

D.O.B. (date of birth):

ADDRESS:

EMAIL ADDRESS:

NOTES:

NAME:

PHONE No.:   BACKGROUND CHECKED: Yes / No

D.O.B. (date of birth):

ADDRESS:

EMAIL ADDRESS:

NOTES:

Co LEADERS AND VOLUNTEERS

NAME:

PHONE No.:   BACKGROUND CHECKED: Yes / No

D.O.B. (date of birth):

ADDRESS:

EMAIL ADDRESS:

NOTES:

NAME:

PHONE No.:   BACKGROUND CHECKED: Yes / No

D.O.B. (date of birth):

ADDRESS:

EMAIL ADDRESS:

NOTES:

NAME:

PHONE No.:   BACKGROUND CHECKED: Yes / No

D.O.B. (date of birth):

ADDRESS:

EMAIL ADDRESS:

NOTES:

NAME:

PHONE No.:   BACKGROUND CHECKED: Yes / No

D.O.B. (date of birth):

ADDRESS:

EMAIL ADDRESS:

NOTES:

🦉 🦉 🦉 TROOP ROSTER

GIRL'S NAME:

PHONE No.:   SCHOOL:

ADDRESS:

EMAIL ADDRESS: T-SHIRT SIZE:

ALLERGIES: AGE: BIRTHDAY:

PARENT'S NAME: PHONE No.:

PARENT'S NAME: PHONE No.:

NOTES:

GIRL'S NAME:

PHONE No.:   SCHOOL:

ADDRESS:

EMAIL ADDRESS: T-SHIRT SIZE:

ALLERGIES: AGE: BIRTHDAY:

PARENT'S NAME: PHONE No.:

PARENT'S NAME: PHONE No.:

NOTES:

GIRL'S NAME:

PHONE No.:   SCHOOL:

ADDRESS:

EMAIL ADDRESS: T-SHIRT SIZE:

ALLERGIES: AGE: BIRTHDAY:

PARENT'S NAME: PHONE No.:

PARENT'S NAME: PHONE No.:

NOTES:

GIRL'S NAME:

PHONE No.:   SCHOOL:

ADDRESS:

EMAIL ADDRESS: T-SHIRT SIZE:

ALLERGIES: AGE: BIRTHDAY:

PARENT'S NAME: PHONE No.:

PARENT'S NAME: PHONE No.:

NOTES:

TROOP ROSTER

GIRL'S NAME:

PHONE No.:   SCHOOL:

ADDRESS:

EMAIL ADDRESS: T-SHIRT SIZE:

ALLERGIES: AGE: BIRTHDAY:

PARENT'S NAME: PHONE No.:

PARENT'S NAME: PHONE No.:

NOTES:

GIRL'S NAME:

PHONE No.:   SCHOOL:

ADDRESS:

EMAIL ADDRESS: T-SHIRT SIZE:

ALLERGIES: AGE: BIRTHDAY:

PARENT'S NAME: PHONE No.:

PARENT'S NAME: PHONE No.:

NOTES:

GIRL'S NAME:

PHONE No.:   SCHOOL:

ADDRESS:

EMAIL ADDRESS: T-SHIRT SIZE:

ALLERGIES: AGE: BIRTHDAY:

PARENT'S NAME: PHONE No.:

PARENT'S NAME: PHONE No.:

NOTES:

GIRL'S NAME:

PHONE No.:   SCHOOL:

ADDRESS:

EMAIL ADDRESS: T-SHIRT SIZE:

ALLERGIES: AGE: BIRTHDAY:

PARENT'S NAME: PHONE No.:

PARENT'S NAME: PHONE No.:

NOTES:

🦉 🦉 🦉 TROOP ROSTER

GIRL'S NAME:

PHONE No.:   SCHOOL:

ADDRESS:

EMAIL ADDRESS: T-SHIRT SIZE:

ALLERGIES: AGE: BIRTHDAY:

PARENT'S NAME: PHONE No.:

PARENT'S NAME: PHONE No.:

NOTES:

GIRL'S NAME:

PHONE No.:   SCHOOL:

ADDRESS:

EMAIL ADDRESS: T-SHIRT SIZE:

ALLERGIES: AGE: BIRTHDAY:

PARENT'S NAME: PHONE No.:

PARENT'S NAME: PHONE No.:

NOTES:

GIRL'S NAME:

PHONE No.:   SCHOOL:

ADDRESS:

EMAIL ADDRESS: T-SHIRT SIZE:

ALLERGIES: AGE: BIRTHDAY:

PARENT'S NAME: PHONE No.:

PARENT'S NAME: PHONE No.:

NOTES:

GIRL'S NAME:

PHONE No.:   SCHOOL:

ADDRESS:

EMAIL ADDRESS: T-SHIRT SIZE:

ALLERGIES: AGE: BIRTHDAY:

PARENT'S NAME: PHONE No.:

PARENT'S NAME: PHONE No.:

NOTES:

TROOP ROSTER 🦉 🦉 🦉

GIRL'S NAME:

PHONE No.:   SCHOOL:

ADDRESS:

EMAIL ADDRESS: T-SHIRT SIZE:

ALLERGIES: AGE: BIRTHDAY:

PARENT'S NAME: PHONE No.:

PARENT'S NAME: PHONE No.:

NOTES:

GIRL'S NAME:

PHONE No.:   SCHOOL:

ADDRESS:

EMAIL ADDRESS: T-SHIRT SIZE:

ALLERGIES: AGE: BIRTHDAY:

PARENT'S NAME: PHONE No.:

PARENT'S NAME: PHONE No.:

NOTES:

GIRL'S NAME:

PHONE No.:   SCHOOL:

ADDRESS:

EMAIL ADDRESS: T-SHIRT SIZE:

ALLERGIES: AGE: BIRTHDAY:

PARENT'S NAME: PHONE No.:

PARENT'S NAME: PHONE No.:

NOTES:

GIRL'S NAME:

PHONE No.:   SCHOOL:

ADDRESS:

EMAIL ADDRESS: T-SHIRT SIZE:

ALLERGIES: AGE: BIRTHDAY:

PARENT'S NAME: PHONE No.:

PARENT'S NAME: PHONE No.:

NOTES:

EMAIL SHEET

PARENT'S NAME	EMAIL

EMAIL SHEET ||||||||||||||||||||||||||||||||||||||||||||||||||||

PARENT'S NAME	EMAIL

HEALTH INFO

GIRLS' NAMES	BLOOD TYPE	HEALTH ISSUES	NOTES

HEALTH INFO

GIRLS' NAMES	BLOOD TYPE	HEALTH ISSUES	NOTES

BIRTHDAY TRACKER

JANUARY

FEBRUARY

MARCH

APRIL

MAY

JUNE

happy Birthday!!

BIRTHDAY TRACKER

JULY	AUGUST	SEPTEMBER

OCTOBER	NOVEMBER	DECEMBER

JANUARY 20__

Mon	Tue	Wed	Thu	Fri	Sat	Sun
–	–	–	–	–	–	–
–	–	–	–	–	–	–
–	–	–	–	–	–	–
–	–	–	–	–	–	–
–	–	–	–	–	–	–

FEBRUARY 20__

Mon	Tue	Wed	Thu	Fri	Sat	Sun
—	—	—	—	—	—	—
—	—	—	—	—	—	—
—	—	—	—	—	—	—
—	—	—	—	—	—	—
—	—	—	—	—	—	—

MARCH 20__

Mon	Tue	Wed	Thu	Fri	Sat	Sun
–	–	–	–	–	–	–
–	–	–	–	–	–	–
–	–	–	–	–	–	–
–	–	–	–	–	–	–
–	–	–	–	–	–	–

APRIL 20__

Mon	Tue	Wed	Thu	Fri	Sat	Sun
–	–	–	–	–	–	–
–	–	–	–	–	–	–
–	–	–	–	–	–	–
–	–	–	–	–	–	–
–	–	–	–	–	–	–

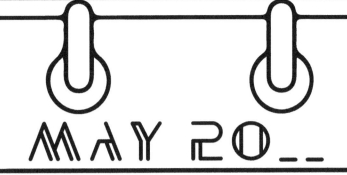

MAY 20__

Mon	Tue	Wed	Thu	Fri	Sat	Sun
–	–	–	–	–	–	–
–	–	–	–	–	–	–
–	–	–	–	–	–	–
–	–	–	–	–	–	–
–	–	–	–	–	–	–

JUNE 20__

Mon	Tue	Wed	Thu	Fri	Sat	Sun
–	–	–	–	–	–	–
–	–	–	–	–	–	–
–	–	–	–	–	–	–
–	–	–	–	–	–	–
–	–	–	–	–	–	–

JULY 20__

Mon	Tue	Wed	Thu	Fri	Sat	Sun
–	–	–	–	–	–	–
–	–	–	–	–	–	–
–	–	–	–	–	–	–
–	–	–	–	–	–	–
–	–	–	–	–	–	–

AUGUST 20__

Mon	Tue	Wed	Thu	Fri	Sat	Sun
–	–	–	–	–	–	–
–	–	–	–	–	–	–
–	–	–	–	–	–	–
–	–	–	–	–	–	–
–	–	–	–	–	–	–

SEPTEMBER 20__

Mon	Tue	Wed	Thu	Fri	Sat	Sun
–	–	–	–	–	–	–
–	–	–	–	–	–	–
–	–	–	–	–	–	–
–	–	–	–	–	–	–
–	–	–	–	–	–	–

23

OCTOBER 20__

Mon	Tue	Wed	Thu	Fri	Sat	Sun
_	_	_	_	_	_	_
_	_	_	_	_	_	_
_	_	_	_	_	_	_
_	_	_	_	_	_	_
_	_	_	_	_	_	_

NOVEMBER 20__

Mon	Tue	Wed	Thu	Fri	Sat	Sun
–	–	–	–	–	–	–
–	–	–	–	–	–	–
–	–	–	–	–	–	–
–	–	–	–	–	–	–
–	–	–	–	–	–	–

DECEMBER 20__

Mon	Tue	Wed	Thu	Fri	Sat	Sun
–	–	–	–	–	–	–
–	–	–	–	–	–	–
–	–	–	–	–	–	–
–	–	–	–	–	–	–
–	–	–	–	–	–	–

JANUARY 20__

Mon	Tue	Wed	Thu	Fri	Sat	Sun
–	–	–	–	–	–	–
–	–	–	–	–	–	–
–	–	–	–	–	–	–
–	–	–	–	–	–	–
–	–	–	–	–	–	–

FEBRUARY 20__

Mon	Tue	Wed	Thu	Fri	Sat	Sun
–	–	–	–	–	–	–
–	–	–	–	–	–	–
–	–	–	–	–	–	–
–	–	–	–	–	–	–
–	–	–	–	–	–	–

MARCH 20__

Mon	Tue	Wed	Thu	Fri	Sat	Sun
–	–	–	–	–	–	–
–	–	–	–	–	–	–
–	–	–	–	–	–	–
–	–	–	–	–	–	–
–	–	–	–	–	–	–

APRIL 20__

Mon	Tue	Wed	Thu	Fri	Sat	Sun
–	–	–	–	–	–	–
–	–	–	–	–	–	–
–	–	–	–	–	–	–
–	–	–	–	–	–	–
–	–	–	–	–	–	–

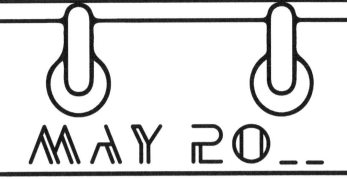

MAY 20__

Mon	Tue	Wed	Thu	Fri	Sat	Sun
–	–	–	–	–	–	–
–	–	–	–	–	–	–
–	–	–	–	–	–	–
–	–	–	–	–	–	–
–	–	–	–	–		

JUNE 20__

Mon	Tue	Wed	Thu	Fri	Sat	Sun
_	_	_	_	_	_	_
_	_	_	_	_	_	_
_	_	_	_	_	_	_
_	_	_	_	_	_	_
_	_	_	_	_	_	_

JULY 20__

Mon	Tue	Wed	Thu	Fri	Sat	Sun
–	–	–	–	–	–	–
–	–	–	–	–	–	–
–	–	–	–	–	–	–
–	–	–	–	–	–	–
–	–	–	–	–	–	–

AUGUST 20__

Mon	Tue	Wed	Thu	Fri	Sat	Sun
–	–	–	–	–	–	–
–	–	–	–	–	–	–
–	–	–	–	–	–	–
–	–	–	–	–	–	–
–	–	–	–	–	–	–

ATTENDANCE TRACKER

DATE	MEETING / EVENT	GIRLS' NAMES											

ATTENDANCE TRACKER

DATE	MEETING / EVENT	GIRLS' NAMES											

ATTENDANCE TRACKER

DATE	MEETING / EVENT	GIRLS' NAMES											

ATTENDANCE TRACKER

DATE	MEETING / EVENT	GIRLS' NAMES												

20__ MEETING EVENT CALENDAR 20__

JANUARY	FEBRUARY	JANUARY	FEBRUARY
MARCH	APRIL	MARCH	APRIL
MAY	JUNE	MAY	JUNE
JULY	AUGUST	JULY	AUGUST
SEPTEMBER	OCTOBER	SEPTEMBER	OCTOBER
NOVEMBER	DECEMBER	NOVEMBER	DECEMBER

MEETING PLANNING SHEET

DATE: PLACE:

	TIME	EVENT	LEADER	SUPPLIES
preparation				
opening				
business				
activity				
activity				
activity				
clean-up closing				
notes				

MEETING PLANNING SHEET

DATE: PLACE:

	TIME	EVENT	LEADER	SUPPLIES
preparation				
opening				
business				
activity				
activity				
activity				
clean-up closing				
notes				

MEETING PLANNING SHEET

DATE: PLACE:

	TIME	EVENT	LEADER	SUPPLIES
preparation				
opening				
business				
activity				
activity				
activity				
clean-up closing				
notes				

MEETING PLANNING SHEET

DATE: PLACE:

	TIME	EVENT	LEADER	SUPPLIES
preparation				
opening				
business				
activity				
activity				
activity				
clean-up closing				
notes				

MEETING PLANNING SHEET

DATE: PLACE:

	TIME	EVENT	LEADER	SUPPLIES
preparation				
opening				
business				
activity				
activity				
activity				
clean-up closing				
notes				

MEETING PLANNING SHEET

DATE: _____ PLACE: _____

	TIME	EVENT	LEADER	SUPPLIES
preparation				
opening				
business				
activity				
activity				
activity				
clean-up closing				
notes				

MEETING PLANNING SHEET

DATE: PLACE:

	TIME	EVENT	LEADER	SUPPLIES
preparation				
opening				
business				
activity				
activity				
activity				
clean-up closing				
notes				

MEETING PLANNING SHEET

DATE: PLACE:

	TIME	EVENT	LEADER	SUPPLIES
preparation				
opening				
business				
activity				
activity				
activity				
clean-up closing				
notes				

MEETING PLANNING SHEET

DATE: PLACE:

	TIME	EVENT	LEADER	SUPPLIES
preparation				
opening				
business				
activity				
activity				
activity				
clean-up closing				
notes				

MEETING PLANNING SHEET

DATE: PLACE:

	TIME	EVENT	LEADER	SUPPLIES
preparation				
opening				
business				
activity				
activity				
activity				
clean-up closing				
notes				

MEETING PLANNING SHEET

DATE: PLACE:

	TIME	EVENT	LEADER	SUPPLIES
preparation				
opening				
business				
activity				
activity				
activity				
clean-up closing				
notes				

MEETING PLANNING SHEET

DATE: PLACE:

	TIME	EVENT	LEADER	SUPPLIES
preparation				
opening				
business				
activity				
activity				
activity				
clean-up closing				
notes				

MEETING PLANNING SHEET

DATE: PLACE:

	TIME	EVENT	LEADER	SUPPLIES
preparation				
opening				
business				
activity				
activity				
activity				
clean-up closing				
notes				

MEETING PLANNING SHEET

DATE: PLACE:

	TIME	EVENT	LEADER	SUPPLIES
preparation				
opening				
business				
activity				
activity				
activity				
clean-up closing				
notes				

MEETING PLANNING SHEET

DATE: PLACE:

	TIME	EVENT	LEADER	SUPPLIES
preparation				
opening				
business				
activity				
activity				
activity				
clean-up closing				
notes				

MEETING PLANNING SHEET

DATE: PLACE:

	TIME	EVENT	LEADER	SUPPLIES
preparation				
opening				
business				
activity				
activity				
activity				
clean-up closing				
notes				

MEETING PLANNING SHEET

DATE: PLACE:

	TIME	EVENT	LEADER	SUPPLIES
preparation				
opening				
business				
activity				
activity				
activity				
clean-up closing				
notes				

MEETING PLANNING SHEET

DATE: PLACE:

	TIME	EVENT	LEADER	SUPPLIES
preparation				
opening				
business				
activity				
activity				
activity				
clean-up closing				
notes				

MEETING PLANNING SHEET

DATE: PLACE:

	TIME	EVENT	LEADER	SUPPLIES
preparation				
opening				
business				
activity				
activity				
activity				
clean-up closing				
notes				

MEETING PLANNING SHEET

DATE: PLACE:

	TIME	EVENT	LEADER	SUPPLIES
preparation				
opening				
business				
activity				
activity				
activity				
clean-up closing				
notes				

MEETING PLANNING SHEET

DATE: _____ PLACE: _____

	TIME	EVENT	LEADER	SUPPLIES
preparation				
opening				
business				
activity				
activity				
activity				
clean-up closing				
notes				

MEETING PLANNING SHEET

DATE: PLACE:

	TIME	EVENT	LEADER	SUPPLIES
preparation				
opening				
business				
activity				
activity				
activity				
clean-up closing				
notes				

MEETING PLANNING SHEET

DATE: PLACE:

	TIME	EVENT	LEADER	SUPPLIES
preparation				
opening				
business				
activity				
activity				
activity				
clean-up closing				
notes				

MEETING PLANNING SHEET

DATE: PLACE:

	TIME	EVENT	LEADER	SUPPLIES
preparation				
opening				
business				
activity				
activity				
activity				
clean-up closing				
notes				

MEETING PLANNING SHEET

DATE: PLACE:

	TIME	EVENT	LEADER	SUPPLIES
preparation				
opening				
business				
activity				
activity				
activity				
clean-up closing				
notes				

MEETING PLANNING SHEET

DATE: _____ PLACE: _____

	TIME	EVENT	LEADER	SUPPLIES
preparation				
opening				
business				
activity				
activity				
activity				
clean-up closing				
notes				

MEETING PLANNING SHEET

DATE: PLACE:

	TIME	EVENT	LEADER	SUPPLIES
preparation				
opening				
business				
activity				
activity				
activity				
clean-up closing				
notes				

MEETING PLANNING SHEET

DATE: PLACE:

	TIME	EVENT	LEADER	SUPPLIES
preparation				
opening				
business				
activity				
activity				
activity				
clean-up closing				
notes				

MEETING PLANNING SHEET

DATE:		PLACE:		
	TIME	EVENT	LEADER	SUPPLIES
preparation				
opening				
business				
activity				
activity				
activity				
clean-up closing				
notes				

MEETING PLANNING SHEET

DATE: _____ PLACE: _____

	TIME	EVENT	LEADER	SUPPLIES
preparation				
opening				
business				
activity				
activity				
activity				
clean-up closing				
notes				

BADGE & PATCH TRACKER

Date:	Badge & Patch Description	Girls' Names:									

BADGE & PATCH TRACKER

Date:	Badge & Patch Description	Girls' Names:														

FORMS & PAPERWORK TRACKER

Date:	Forms or Paperwork To Be Done	Girls' Names:										

FORMS & PAPERWORK TRACKER

Date:	Forms or Paperwork To Be Done	Girls' Names:															

TROOP DUES & FEES TRACKER

Date:	Description (Membership Dues, Uniform, Field Trips Fees etc.)	Girls' Names: (Mark When Paid)										

TROOP DUES & FEES TRACKER

Date:	Description (Membership Dues, Uniform, Field Trips Fees etc.)	Girls' Names:												

TROOP DUES & FEES TRACKER

Date:	Description (Membership Dues, Uniform, Field Trips Fees etc.)	Girls' Names: (Mark When Paid)										

TROOP DUES & FEES TRACKER

Date:	Description (Membership Dues, Uniform, Field Trips Fees etc.)	Girls' Names:																

FINANCIAL LEDGER

DATE	DESCRIPTION	INCOME $	EXPENSE $	BALANCE $

FINANCIAL LEDGER

DATE	DESCRIPTION	INCOME $	EXPENSE $	BALANCE $

FINANCIAL LEDGER

DATE	DESCRIPTION	INCOME $	EXPENSE $	BALANCE $

FINANCIAL LEDGER

DATE	DESCRIPTION	INCOME $	EXPENSE $	BALANCE $

CHECKING ACCOUNT TRACKER

Bank Name: **Address:**

Phone Number: **Hours of Operation:**

Account Number: **Routing Number:**

DATE	TRANSACTION	WITHDRAWAL	DEPOSIT	BALANCE

CHECKING ACCOUNT TRACKER

Bank Name: **Address:**

Phone Number: **Hours of Operation:**

Account Number: **Routing Number:**

DATE	TRANSACTION	WITHDRAWAL	DEPOSIT	BALANCE

CHECKING ACCOUNT TRACKER

Bank Name: **Address:**

Phone Number: **Hours of Operation:**

Account Number: **Routing Number:**

DATE	TRANSACTION	WITHDRAWAL	DEPOSIT	BALANCE

CHECKING ACCOUNT TRACKER

Bank Name: **Address:**

Phone Number: **Hours of Operation:**

Account Number: **Routing Number:**

DATE	TRANSACTION	WITHDRAWAL	DEPOSIT	BALANCE

INDIVIDUAL GIRLS' PRODUCT SALES TRACKER

Date:	Product	Girls' Names											

INDIVIDUAL GIRLS' PRODUCT SALES TRACKER

Date:	Product	Girls' Names

INDIVIDUAL GIRLS' PRODUCT SALES TRACKER

Date:	Product	Girls' Names									

INDIVIDUAL GIRLS' PRODUCT SALES TRACKER

Date:	Product	Girls' Names

INDIVIDUAL GIRLS' PRODUCT SALES TRACKER

Date:	Product	Girls' Names												

INDIVIDUAL GIRLS' PRODUCT SALES TRACKER

Date:	Product	Girls' Names

BOOTH SALES TRACKER

BOOTH LOCATION: DATE:

Product Name							
Price Per Box							
No. of Boxes at the Start							
No. of Boxes at the End							
Total No. of Boxes Sold							
Total $ Earned							

GIRL'S NAME:	STARTING TIME	END TIME:	No. OF HOURS	No. OF BOXES SOLD

Total No. of Boxes Sold: **Starting Cash Amount:**

                                          Ending Cash Amount:

$ $ in Donations: **Credit Card Sales:**

TOTAL BOOTH SALES PROFIT:

BOOTH SALES TRACKER

BOOTH LOCATION: DATE:

Product Name						
Price Per Box						
No. of Boxes at the Start						
No. of Boxes at the End						
Total No. of Boxes Sold						
Total $ Earned						

GIRL'S NAME:	STARTING TIME	END TIME:	No. OF HOURS	No. OF BOXES SOLD

Total No. of Boxes Sold: **Starting Cash Amount:**

                                                 Ending Cash Amount:

$ $ in Donations:

                                                  Credit Card Sales:

TOTAL BOOTH SALES PROFIT:

BOOTH SALES TRACKER

BOOTH LOCATION: DATE:

Product Name						
Price Per Box						
No. of Boxes at the Start						
No. of Boxes at the End						
Total No. of Boxes Sold						
Total $ Earned						

GIRL'S NAME:	STARTING TIME	END TIME:	No. OF HOURS	No. OF BOXES SOLD

Total No. of Boxes Sold: **Starting Cash Amount:**

                                     Ending Cash Amount:

$ $ in Donations:

                                     Credit Card Sales:

TOTAL BOOTH SALES PROFIT:

BOOTH SALES TRACKER

BOOTH LOCATION: DATE:

Product Name							
Price Per Box							
No. of Boxes at the Start							
No. of Boxes at the End							
Total No. of Boxes Sold							
Total $ Earned							

GIRL'S NAME:	STARTING TIME	END TIME:	No. OF HOURS	No. OF BOXES SOLD

Total No. of Boxes Sold: **Starting Cash Amount:**

                                    Ending Cash Amount:

$ $ in Donations: **Credit Card Sales:**

TOTAL BOOTH SALES PROFIT:

BOOTH SALES TRACKER

BOOTH LOCATION: DATE:

Product Name							
Price Per Box							
No. of Boxes at the Start							
No. of Boxes at the End							
Total No. of Boxes Sold							
Total $ Earned							

GIRL'S NAME:	STARTING TIME	END TIME:	No. OF HOURS	No. OF BOXES SOLD

Total No. of Boxes Sold:

$ $ in Donations:

Starting Cash Amount:

Ending Cash Amount:

Credit Card Sales:

TOTAL BOOTH SALES PROFIT:

BOOTH SALES TRACKER

BOOTH LOCATION: DATE:

Product Name						
Price Per Box						
No. of Boxes at the Start						
No. of Boxes at the End						
Total No. of Boxes Sold						
Total $ Earned						

GIRL'S NAME:	STARTING TIME	END TIME:	No. OF HOURS	No. OF BOXES SOLD

Total No. of Boxes Sold: **Starting Cash Amount:**

                                 Ending Cash Amount:

$ $ in Donations: **Credit Card Sales:**

TOTAL BOOTH SALES PROFIT:

BOOTH SALES TRACKER

BOOTH LOCATION: DATE:

Product Name							
Price Per Box							
No. of Boxes at the Start							
No. of Boxes at the End							
Total No. of Boxes Sold							
Total $ Earned							

GIRL'S NAME:	STARTING TIME	END TIME:	No. OF HOURS	No. OF BOXES SOLD

Total No. of Boxes Sold: **Starting Cash Amount:**

                                   Ending Cash Amount:

$ $ in Donations: **Credit Card Sales:**

TOTAL BOOTH SALES PROFIT:

BOOTH SALES TRACKER

BOOTH LOCATION: DATE:

Product Name						
Price Per Box						
No. of Boxes at the Start						
No. of Boxes at the End						
Total No. of Boxes Sold						
Total $ Earned						

GIRL'S NAME:	STARTING TIME	END TIME:	No. OF HOURS	No. OF BOXES SOLD

Total No. of Boxes Sold: **Starting Cash Amount:**

                                        Ending Cash Amount:

$ $ in Donations: **Credit Card Sales:**

TOTAL BOOTH SALES PROFIT:

BOOTH SALES TRACKER

BOOTH LOCATION: _____ DATE: _____

Product Name							
Price Per Box							
No. of Boxes at the Start							
No. of Boxes at the End							
Total No. of Boxes Sold							
Total $ Earned							

GIRL'S NAME:	STARTING TIME	END TIME:	No. OF HOURS	No. OF BOXES SOLD

Total No. of Boxes Sold: _____

$ $ in Donations: _____

Starting Cash Amount: _____

Ending Cash Amount: _____

Credit Card Sales: _____

TOTAL BOOTH SALES PROFIT:

BOOTH SALES TRACKER

BOOTH LOCATION: DATE:

Product Name						
Price Per Box						
No. of Boxes at the Start						
No. of Boxes at the End						
Total No. of Boxes Sold						
Total $ Earned						

GIRL'S NAME:	STARTING TIME	END TIME:	No. OF HOURS	No. OF BOXES SOLD

Total No. of Boxes Sold: **Starting Cash Amount:**

                                              Ending Cash Amount:

$ $ in Donations: **Credit Card Sales:**

TOTAL BOOTH SALES PROFIT:

BOOTH SALES TRACKER

BOOTH LOCATION: DATE:

Product Name							
Price Per Box							
No. of Boxes at the Start							
No. of Boxes at the End							
Total No. of Boxes Sold							
Total $ Earned							

GIRL'S NAME:	STARTING TIME	END TIME:	No. OF HOURS	No. OF BOXES SOLD

Total No. of Boxes Sold:

$ $ in Donations:

Starting Cash Amount:

Ending Cash Amount:

Credit Card Sales:

TOTAL BOOTH SALES PROFIT:

BOOTH SALES TRACKER

BOOTH LOCATION: DATE:

Product Name						
Price Per Box						
No. of Boxes at the Start						
No. of Boxes at the End						
Total No. of Boxes Sold						
Total $ Earned						

GIRL'S NAME:	STARTING TIME	END TIME:	No. OF HOURS	No. OF BOXES SOLD

Total No. of Boxes Sold: **Starting Cash Amount:**

                               Ending Cash Amount:

$ $ in Donations: **Credit Card Sales:**

TOTAL BOOTH SALES PROFIT:

SNACK SIGNUP SHEET

MEETING DATE	GIRL'S NAME	NOTES

SNACK SIGNUP SHEET

MEETING DATE	GIRL'S NAME	NOTES

VOLUNTEER SIGNUP SHEET

EVENT DATE	DESCRIPTION OF EVENT	VOLUNTEERS

VOLUNTEER SIGNUP SHEET

EVENT DATE	DESCRIPTION OF EVENT	VOLUNTEERS

VOLUNTEER SIGNUP SHEET

EVENT DATE	DESCRIPTION OF EVENT	VOLUNTEERS

VOLUNTEER SIGNUP SHEET

EVENT DATE	DESCRIPTION OF EVENT	VOLUNTEERS

NOTES & TO-DO LIST

NOTES	DATE:

NOTES	DATE:

NOTES & TO-DO LIST

NOTES	DATE:

NOTES	DATE:

NOTES & TO-DO LIST

NOTES	DATE:

NOTES	DATE:

NOTES & TO-DO LIST

NOTES	DATE:

NOTES	DATE:

NOTES & TO-DO LIST

NOTES	DATE:

NOTES	DATE:

NOTES & TO-DO LIST

NOTES	DATE:

NOTES	DATE:

NOTES & TO-DO LIST

NOTES	DATE:

NOTES	DATE:

NOTES & TO-DO LIST

NOTES	DATE:

NOTES	DATE:

NOTES & TO-DO LIST

NOTES	DATE:

NOTES	DATE:

NOTES & TO-DO LIST

NOTES	DATE:

NOTES	DATE:

NOTES & TO-DO LIST

NOTES	DATE:

NOTES	DATE:

NOTES & TO-DO LIST

NOTES	DATE:

NOTES	DATE:

NOTES & TO-DO LIST

NOTES	DATE:

NOTES	DATE:

NOTES & TO-DO LIST

NOTES	DATE:

NOTES	DATE:

NOTES & TO-DO LIST

NOTES	DATE:

NOTES	DATE:

NOTES & TO-DO LIST

NOTES	DATE:

NOTES	DATE:

NOTES & TO-DO LIST

NOTES	DATE:

NOTES	DATE:

NOTES & TO-DO LIST

NOTES	DATE:

NOTES	DATE:

NOTES & TO-DO LIST

NOTES	DATE:

NOTES	DATE:

NOTES & TO-DO LIST

NOTES	DATE:

NOTES	DATE:

Made in the USA
Las Vegas, NV
24 September 2021